god + the arts

FINDING THE LARGER STORY
THROUGH MUSIC

SIX SMALL GROUP STUDIES USING THE GREAT SONGS

GOD AND THE ARTS
Finding the Larger Story through Music
© 2008 Serendipity House

Published by Serendipity House Publishers, Nashville, Tennessee

ISBN: 978-1-5749-4420-4
Item No. 005117804

Dewey Decimal Classification: 791.43
Subject Headings: POPULAR MUSIC—RELIGIOUS ASPECTS

Scripture quotations marked HCSB are taken from the *Holman Christian Standard Bible®*, Copyright © 1999, 2000, 2002, 2003 by Holman Bible Publishers. Used by permission.

Scriptures marked *The Message* are taken from *The Message®*. Copyright © 1993, 1994, 1995, 1996, 2000, 2001, 2002. Used by permission of NavPress Publishing Group.

Scriptures marked NIV are taken from the *Holy Bible, New International Version*, Copyright © 1973, 1978, 1984 by International Bible Society. Used by permission.

Scripture quotations marked (NLT) are taken from the Holy Bible, New Living Translation, copyright © 1996. Used by permission of Tyndale House Publishers, Inc., Wheaton, IL 60189 USA. All rights reserved.

Scriptures marked NASB are taken from the *New American Standard Bible®*, Copyright © 1960, 1962, 1963, 1968, 1971, 1972, 1973, 1975, 1977, 1995 by the Lockman Foundation. Used by permission. (www.lockman.org)

To purchase Serendipity House resources:
ORDER ONLINE   www.SerendipityHouse.com
WRITE   Serendipity House, 117 10th Avenue North, Nashville, TN 37234
FAX   (615) 277-8181
PHONE   (800) 525-9563

ALSO IN THE GOD AND THE ARTS SERIES:
Finding Redemption in the Movies   ISBN 978-1-5749-4342-9
Finding Jesus in the Movies   ISBN 978-1-5749-4355-9

1-800-525-9563 • www.SerendipityHouse.com

Printed in the United States of America

CONTENTS

INTRODUCTION

> I have no pleasure in any man who despises music. It is no invention of ours: it is a gift of God. I place it next to theology. Satan hates music: he knows how it drives the evil spirit out of us.
>
> **MARTIN LUTHER**

> Music and rhythm find their way into the secret places of the soul.
>
> **PLATO**

THE LARGER STORY

> He has also set eternity in the hearts of men...
>
> **ECCLESIASTES 3:11**

Ecclesiastes 3:11 suggests that we come ready-made to understand the greatest story, the epic story, of betrayal and an enemy, of the fight between the destroyer and the redeemer, of something lost and the journey to recovery, of a hero and ultimate restoration. The Larger Story is the story of the gospel and Scripture provides the backstory, the truth behind the stories that move us.

In the beginning—during the time before time—there was perfect fellowship among the Triune Godhead and the angelic beings that He created. Act I of the Larger Story includes perfection and harmony and it describes beauty, mystery, and order. Act II begins as pride enters the arch-angel Lucifer's heart. Evil enters the story and with it the Villain. Lucifer rebels, he becomes known as Satan, order is tainted, and the villain is expelled from the heavenly realm with his followers.

Genesis 1 begins Act III of the Great Story as the dust still settles from the great war. Act III accounts for most of the Bible and human history. Act III includes the Hero—Redeemer's daring, redemptive mission and climaxes with the cross and His resurrection. Act III continues through today and will continue until the ultimate restoration and paradise regained in Act IV.

Stories, great and small, share the same essential structure because the weighty stories of our time borrow their power from a Larger Story. What we sense stirring within is a heart that is made for a place in the Larger Story. What is it about these powerful stories that make us weep, make us laugh, and make our hearts come alive? Is it not that these stories borrow from THE STORY—the Epic Story. Great movies, great books, and great songs speak to us because they hint at or tell a story, and story is the language of the heart.

Finding the Larger Story through Music is the third release in the God and the Arts small-group Bible study series. The experience has been created to guide you on a journey into the deepest place—your heart. On this expedition you'll begin to realize that the great Epic, the story of the Bible, is already alive and placed within this part of who you are as a spiritual being. You'll find that your heart is the place with the most capacity for hearing God. During this experience you can expect to explore six themes of the Larger Story: Void, Desire, Lament, Freedom, Justice, and Romance.

Music is more and more accessible than ever before and has become one of the primary languages of the heart. It makes sense that insightful songwriters would write songs that hint at, or even retell, the Larger Story. Sure, there are transcendent paintings, poems, and films—but when we understand the spiritual component of music, we quickly understand how it finds it's way "into the secret places of the soul."

THE SPIRITUAL COMPONENT OF MUSIC
Music is a creation of God. We can see in Scripture that there was music in Heaven before creation. Given the song of the angels in various places, we assume that there will be music in Heaven—eternally. We can hear it, we can feel it, but we can't see it.

Of couse there is "throw-away" music just as there are "throw-away" books. But when all the elements of a good song are in place , the song becomes so much greater than the simple sum of its elements. There are those writers, composers, and singers who touch the epic alive within us. These are the skilled musicians in touch with the eternity in their hearts. They may not call themselves Christian or even spiritual, but they are spiritual creations of a creative God nonetheless. God is certainly capable of using the everyday to communicate the eternal, the common to reveal the Story—His Epic.

Why is it that at times a three-minute song can do more for our soul than a 300-page book? Or even a passage of Scripture? It could be that because God has put "eternity in our hearts" we recognize elements of the Larger Story in the timeless music of our culture. In these moments our heart is in tune with the loss of Eden, the freedom that awaits those that proclaim Christ, and the justice inherent in the heart of God.

EXPECTATION

- Experience God through music (Psalm 150)
- Learn to listen to and treasure your heart (Proverbs 4:23)
- As your heart awakens and begins to speak, you may be surprised at what it reveals to you. Our deepest-held beliefs may not be what we think or say we believe (Psalm 51:6)
- Listen for the call of the crucial role you have in the Larger Story (Deuteronomy 20:3)

DISCLAIMER

Serendipity House doesn't approve of every song, album, quote, action, or public appearance of the artists you'll be engaging in this Bible study. Often the best stories—even in the Bible—include some pretty unsavory characters and behavior. Even a number of heroes in the Bible displayed some pretty ungodly, unsavory, and questionable behavior. Abraham, Jacob, Rahab, and David come to mind. Please note that these songs aren't always suitable for every situation. This Bible study has not been created for a mix of kids and adults or for kids alone. Maturity is a prerequisite.

BEST USE

Finding the Larger Story through Music has several uses:

1. Good fit for normal breaks between books or other Bible studies
2. Perfect fit for special events or retreats
3. A great 6-week small group study
4. Content suitable for teaching and preaching illustrations
5. Stand-alone conversations for each of the six themes

MADE FOR MORE

Music has always touched us, but as it has become more accessible, its potential to touch us deeply has increased as well. The songs that move us touch a deep embodiment of God inherent to all of us. That is, our hearts recognize something more within the music and the lyrics of the great songs. The Great Story of Scripture can be understood in much the same way. Missing the "music" of the Bible is missing the gospel. Missing they "lyric" of the Bible is to miss the story. They are weaved together to reveal at least in part the depth that is God. The music of the Bible and the lyric of the gospel work in concert to bring the story alive within us.

NAVIGATING FINDING THE LARGER STORY

SETTING THE STAGE   Setting the stage includes a brief introduction, the Set List, and initial conversation starters—usually 2-3 questions.

SET LIST   At every concert, at the feet of the artists, is a list of songs called the Set List. The songs you'll be exploring during each small-group meeting are provided here in the Set List.

BACKSTORY   The backstory of the Larger Story is the story of the Bible—the inspired Word of God. This icon identifies the Scriptures used during the small-group experience. Within the great songs lies the drama of the heart, and your heart has been pre-wired to recognize this drama.

SHEET MUSIC   Sheet music is the heart of the small group experience. Comprised of provocative questions, lyrics, Scripture, and the occasional insight, this part of the meeting is where the Larger Story emerge.s

PUSH PLAY   You can't have a discussion about music without…MUSIC! You may choose to listen to the songs on a CD over a meal or before the small group meets. Or you might want to get through the evening's socializing and save the music until everyone's settled and ready to listen. Or even still, the group can listen informally during a meal or snacks. It's entirely up to the group.

INWARD AND UPWARD   The experience will always end with a prayer time that includes elements from the conversation. Inward and Upward may include questions to take to God or to take to your heart.

REWIND   Rewind lists additional songs that may add to your discussion. Use this time to unpack topics that may have been identified during your time together.

REHEARSAL   Rehearsal looks forward to your next *Finding the Larger Story through Music* conversation. This section includes a brief description of the next experience and accompanying setlist.

NOTES

NOTES

VOID

IN THE WAKE OF EDEN

SETTING THE STAGE

In the Larger Story there is a void left from the loss of Eden—the loss of paradise. Humanity was created to live eternally in harmony with God in the garden of Eden. That's how our hearts were created, pre-wired. We cannot begin to comprehend what was tainted and lost in Genesis 3. Not only was sickness, death, and evil introduced into the world, but according to Scripture even creation is being more or less held back (Rom. 8:19-21).

Although our minds, our cognitive, thinking parts, may not catch references to this part of the Larger Story, our hearts are very alive in the reality that paradise is lost; that this place we find ourselves calling home is a bit of a strange fit.

[1]These are the words of the Teacher, King David's son, who ruled in Jerusalem. [2]"Everything is meaningless," says the Teacher, "utterly meaningless!" [3]What do people get for all their hard work? [4]Generations come and go, but nothing really changes. [5]The sun rises and sets and hurries around to rise again. [6]The wind blows south and north, here and there, twisting back and forth, getting nowhere. [7]The rivers run into the sea, but the sea is never full. Then the water returns again to the rivers and flows again to the sea. [8]Everything is so weary and tiresome! No matter how much we see, we are never satisfied. No matter how much we hear, we are not content.

ECCLESIASTES 1:1-8 (NLT)

1. What language, or specific words, from Ecclesiastes 1:1-8 conjures images of the void left in the loss of Eden?

2. Describe what the writer of Ecclesiastes must have felt as he penned these words.

BEFORE JOINING THE STORY IN SONG:

*   Ask God to speak to you and reveal more of His heart to you in this time.

*   Pay attention to what moves you. Is is the tone of the guitar? The emotion in the vocals? The rhythmic elements?

*   Remember that musical tastes are subjective. We don't all like the same kind of music, so if any from this set list don't seem to be working for you, it's OK. Be patient.

SET LIST

"How Soon is Now?"
The Smiths

"Time"
Pink Floyd

"Running on Empty"
Jackson Browne

"California Dreamin'"
The Mamas and the Papas

FROM THE 1984 ALBUM, HATFUL OF HOLLOW

SHEET MUSIC

"How Soon Is Now?" was a top 20 hit in the UK in 1984, but has gone on to become an iconic hit from the 80s playing in numerous soundtracks and advertisements.

You shut your mouth
how can you say
I go about things the wrong way
I am human and I need to be loved
just like everybody else does

HOW SOON IS NOW?

1. The song says "I am human and I need to be loved." What does this imply? What is missing?

Even the music has a hollow feel to it with its extreme use of reverb and echo. Minor to major chord changes also give it a restless and even exotic feel, just the opposite of the shy and bleak outlook the song expresses. It's as if the music is expressing the singer's ideal while the lyric expresses the reality.

2. What do you think makes a songwriter talk in terms of being "unloved"? And why do you think a song about being unloved would be popular?

3. The phrase "on your own" is repeated in the song. Read Jeremiah 2:13 below. How do you think the lyrics given and Jeremiah 2:13 express the void left by Eden?

4. Both the lyrics and Jeremiah 2:13 touch on our self-referenced nature. How do you think this self-referenced nature contributes to the void we feel?

> ... so you go, and you stand on your own
> and you leave on your own
> and you go home, and you cry
> and you want to die.
>
> **HOW SOON IS NOW?**

> "My people have committed two sins:
> They have forsaken me,
> the spring of living water,
> and have dug their own cisterns,
> broken cisterns that cannot hold water."
>
> **JEREMIAH 2:13 (NIV)**

5. How do you think the loss of Eden has affected our ability to love, or to feel loved?

TIME   Pink Floyd

FROM THE 1973 ALBUM, DARK SIDE OF THE MOON

SHEET MUSIC

The opening of the song contains recording of clocks recorded separately at several antique stores, then layered upon each other in the studio.

It's estimated that 1 in 14 people under the age of 50 own or has owned Pink Floyd's **Dark Side of the Moon,** the mega-platinum selling concept album about the darker sides of the human condition.

> Ticking away the moments that make up a dull day
> You fritter and waste the hours in an off-hand way
> Kicking around on a piece of ground in your home town
> Waiting for someone or something to show you the way
>
> TIME

This is simply a picture of nothingness. The song is written in second person, but the lyrics imply the writer is speaking to himself rather than the listener or another character. The thought is not only that time is being wasted, but it's being wasted on a "dull day."

6.   Refer to the Ecclesiastes passage given on page 12. In what ways do you think "Time" is similar to Ecclesiastes 1:1-8?

7.   What does 2 Thessalonians 3:11-12 below suggest we do with this void? How do you think this works in contrast with what's going on in "Time"?

> [11]For we hear that there are some among you who walk irresponsibly, not working at all, but interfering with the work of others.[12]Now we command and exhort such people, by the Lord Jesus Christ, that quietly working, they may eat their own bread.
>
> 2 THESSALONIANS 3:11-12 (HCSB)

8. The lyrics below refer to being cold and tired. Read Genesis 3:15-16. How do you think the void left by Eden's loss results in conditions like this?

> Home, home again
> I like to be here when I can
> And when I come home cold and tired
> Its good to warm my bones beside the fire
> Far away across the field
> The tolling of the iron bell
> Calls the faithful to their knees
> To hear the softly spoken magic spells.
>
> TIME

> [15] [God] said to the woman: I will intensify your labor pains
> ...[16] And He said to Adam ..."The ground is cursed because
> of you. You will eat from it by means of painful labor"
>
> GENESIS 3:15-16 (HCSB)

RUNNING ON EMPTY   Jackson Browne

FROM THE 1977 ALBUM, RUNNING ON EMPTY

SHEET MUSIC

Everybody runs on empty at some point in their lives. But it's a different experience when our "running" puts us on a road that we don't even recognize, much less gives us direction in life.

9. Do you think the singer/songwriter is aware of any reasons for his running—or has it become a way of life for him? What do you think the lack of intention reveals about the void we feel deep in our hearts?

"Running on Empty" was recorded in five locations, including the stage, three hotels rooms, and a tour bus

Gotta do what you can just to keep your love alive
Trying not to confuse it with what you do to survive
In sixty-nine I was twenty-one and I called the road my own
I don't know when that road turned onto the road I'm on

Running on - running blind
Running on - running into the sun
But I'm running behind
RUNNING ON EMPTY

10. Read 1 Corinthians 9:26-27 below. How do you think this verse indicates that its writer has sensed the void left by Eden's loss?

[26]I don't know about you, but I'm running hard for the finish line. I'm giving it everything I've got. No sloppy living for me! [27]I'm staying alert and in top condition. I'm not going to get caught napping, telling everyone else all about it and then missing out myself.
1 CORINTHIANS 9:26-27 (THE MESSAGE)

11. In what ways do you think "Running on Empty" in on the right track?

Everyone I know, everywhere I go
People need some reason to believe

. . .

I look around for the friends that I used to turn to pull me through
Looking into their eyes I see them running too
RUNNING ON EMPTY

12. In John 10:10 Jesus refers to a thief that comes to kill and destroy. How do you think this thief takes advantage of the void left in our hearts at the loss of Eden? Why do you think this thief, our enemy, would want us to continue on some "unknown" road, running on empty?

> A thief comes only to steal and to kill and to destroy. I have come that they may have life and have it in abundance.
>
> JOHN 10:10 (HCSB)

CALIFORNIA DREAMIN'   The Mamas and the Papas

FROM THE 1970 ALBUM, 16 GREATEST

SHEET MUSIC

13. What kind of image is painted by the lyrics below?

> All the leaves are brown
> And the sky is grey
> I went for a walk
> On a winter's day
> I'd be safe and warm
> If I was in L.A.
> California dreamin'
> On such a winter's day
>
> CALIFORNIA DREAMIN'

14. Of all the places, why do you think the songwriter would pine for California? What assumptions are being drawn about California in this song?

15. Read Psalm 27:4-5 below. What type of deep satisfaction does your heart long for and what do you think this says about the nature of your true desire?

"The one thing I ask of the Lord—the thing I seek most—is to live in the house of the Lord all the days of my life, delighting in the Lord's perfections and meditating in his Temple. For he will conceal me there when troubles come; he will hide me in his sanctuary. He will place me out of reach on a high rock."

PSALM 27:4-5 (NLT)

16. In what ways do you think "California Dreamin" points to Isaiah 43:1-2 below?

[1]Now this is what the LORD says ..."Do not fear, for I have redeemed you; I have called you by your name; you are Mine. [2]I will be with you when you pass through the waters, and when you pass through the rivers, they will not overwhelm you. You will not be scorched when you walk through the fire, and the flame will not burn you.

ISAIAH 43:1-2 (HCSB)

INWARD AND UPWARD

Thank God for establishing a permanent solution to the void left in the wake of Eden.

- Thank God for a redemption powerful enough to restore all that has been lost.
- Thank God for an invitation to join Him in the adventure of life.
- Thank God for the ability to sense the void.

Although a relationship with God through Jesus can fill the void of our lives, remember that your heart will always be able to recognize the void left in the wake Eden's loss. This allows you to acknowledge it for what it is instead of trying to solve this reality with various addictions—from bad habits to destructive behavior. The ability to recognize the void earmarks a heart of flesh's ability to feel and feel powerfully. It also gives you the ability to recognize brokenness and suffering as God works in you and through you for His redemptive purposes.

 ## REWIND

"Wishlist"
Pearl Jam

"Sittin on the Dock of the Bay"
Otis Redding

"Layla"
Derek and the Dominoes

REHEARSAL

During your next *Finding the Larger Story through Music* conversation you'll be taking a look at Desire as it relates to the Larger Story God is revealing. We will define desire as that that makes the heart come alive. There are many imposters of desire and they manifest themselves in our daily lives in various ways. Between now and the next time you get together, try to find time to listen to the following songs. How do they make you feel? How do you think they are supposed to make you feel?

"Still Haven't Found What I'm Looking For"
U2

"Stairway to Heaven"
Led Zeppelin

"More Than a Feeling"
Boston

"Iris"
Goo Goo Dolls

NOTES

DESIRE

CREATED TO BE MORE

II

SETTING THE STAGE

In CS Lewis' *The Screwtape Letters*, an elder demon tells a younger demon that he is mentoring, Your job is to bring me people that do not care. What the elder demon in this case really wants is to get us to a place at which we no longer—or cannot—feel deeply. Our enemy, the adversay, the devil, wants nothing more than to rob us of our desire because desire is the first step in climbing from the void of loss.

Although desire was tainted by the events in the garden of Eden, its place in the Larger Story is crucial to our understanding of what God has created us to be—our giftedness, our passion. These revelations begin with the desire to be more. To neglect the heart's desire is foolish. To kill the heart's desire is suicide. To allow your heart's desire to wander is disaster. Passion has potential to make both great saints ... and great sinners[1]. To fear desire for its potential for evil, however, is to rob desire of any hope for it to do what God wishes for us. During this conversation you'll take a look at several songs exhorting us to be more than what we are.

> A thief comes only to steal and to kill and to destroy. I have come that they may have life and have it in abundance.
>
> **JOHN 10:10 (HCSB)**

1.   Why do you think Jesus would quality life with "and have it in abundance"?

> For everyone who asks receives, and the one who searches finds, and to the one who knocks, the door will be opened.
>
> **MATTHEW 7:8 (HCSB)**

---

[1]Taken from a series of John Eldredge seminars on desire. These seminars can be found and downloaded as podcasts at iTunes.

2.   How do you think Matthew 7:8 could be an invitation to desire?

BEFORE JOINING THE STORY IN SONG:

- Ask God to speak to you and reveal more of His heart to you in this time.

- Pay attention to what moves you. Is is the tone of the guitar? The emotion in the vocals? The rhythmic elements? Be aware of the moments when you feel something more.

- Musical tastes are subjective. We don't all like the same kind of music, but we are all moved by certain circumstances.

SET LIST

"Still Haven't Found What I'm Looking For"
U2

"More Than a Feeling"
Boston

"Stairway to Heaven"
Led Zeppelin

"Iris"
Goo Goo Dolls

I STILL HAVEN'T FOUND WHAT I'M LOOKING FOR   U2

FROM THE 1987 ALBUM, THE JOSHUA TREE

SHEET MUSIC

The Joshua Tree has sold over 25 million copies worldwide and is considered one of the greatest recordings of all time.

U2 lead singer Bono has been known to say that embracing God opens up more questions than it answers.

1. The first few lines of "Still Haven't Found What I'm Looking For" are below. Circle the words that indicate some sort of desperation. Which of these words touch you emotionally?

I have climbed highest mountains
I have run through the fields
Only to be with you
Only to be with you
I have run
I have crawled
I have scaled these city walls
These city walls
Only to be with you

I STILL HAVEN'T FOUND WHAT I'M LOOKING FOR

2. The song describes a process of running, crawling, scaling, and climbing, yet still being unfulfilled. Do you think this is describing a romantic or spiritual desire? Explain.

3. Read Jeremiah 6:13. What kind of healing do you think could be associated with desire? What kind of healing do you think "burns like a fire," as the songs describes?

> I have kissed honey lips
> Felt the healing fingertips
> It burned like a fire
> This burning desire
> **I STILL HAVEN'T FOUND WHAT I'M LOOKING FOR**

> ¹³From prophet to priest, everyone deals falsely. ¹⁴They have treated My people's brokenness superficially, claiming: Peace, peace, when there is no peace.
> **JEREMIAH 6:13-14 (HCSB)**

John 5:1-6 describes a scene at a pool in Bethesda during Jesus' time. Apparently, the blind and lame would wait at the poolside until the water stirred—which indicated that angels would heal the first to the pool. This passage describes a certain man that had been at the pool for some time.

> ⁵One man was there who had been sick for 38 years. ⁶When Jesus saw him lying there and knew he had already been there a long time, He said to him, "Do you want to get well?"
> **JOHN 5:5-6 (HCSB)**

4. Why do you think Jesus asked this question? What do you think Jesus was really asking the paralytic?

> You broke the bonds
> And you loosened the chains
> **I STILL HAVEN'T FOUND WHAT I'M LOOKING FOR**

5. In what ways do you think it's possible to be an emotional paralytic, waiting by a metaphorical pool like the one described in John 5?

6. How do you think Jesus' question in John 5:6 could be directed at an emotional paralytic? What, if anything, could you say about the relationship between desire and "getting well"? What do you think Jesus' question implies about the state of the man's desire?

MORE THAN A FEELING

Boston

FROM THE 1976 ALBUM, BOSTON

SHEET MUSIC

7. How do you think desire can be more than any sort of feeling? How do you think desire can be deeper than "feeling"?

Boston's sound can be recognized by unique guitar work that blends different leads, often alternating between and then mixing electric and acoustic guitars.

8. Both "More Than a Feeling" and Ephesians 5:14 refer to light. While one prompts us to action, the other looks for escape. How do you think desire is present in each case? Absent?

Boston *still ranks as the best-selling debut album in US History*

9. Both also include an awakening. What do you think Ephesians 5:14 asks of you? In this passage, what do you think it means to be a "sleeper"? What about "rise from the dead"?

I looked out this morning and the sun was gone
Turned on some music to start my day
I lost myself in a familiar song
I closed my eyes and I slipped away

MORE THAN A FEELING

for what makes everything clear is light. Therefore it is said: Get up, sleeper, and rise up from the dead, and the Messiah will shine on you.

EPHESIANS 5:14 (HCSB)

10. Why do you think desire would have a part in the Larger Story God is revealing? In your life, what have you tended to do with your heart's desire?

11. How do you think "More Than a Feeling" resolves the desire felt deep inside?

> When I'm tired and thinking cold
> I hide in my music, forget the day
> And dream of a girl I used to know
> I closed my eyes and she slipped away.
> **MORE THAN A FEELING**

12. Look at the last lyrics again. To what sort of desire do you think "More Than a Feeling" defaults? How do you think you could make a distinction between "desire" and "objects of desire"?

13. How do you think temporarily numbing desire differs from the hope offered in Isaiah 65:17?

> "For I will create a new heaven and a new earth; the past events will not be remembered or come to mind."
>
> **ISAIAH 65:17 (HCSB)**

"More Than a Feeling" romanticizes slipping away—suppressing desire—while still acknowledging that's there's got to be more. It's not negative, but it's also not hopeful. Ultimately the song defaults to romantic love before finally giving up and slipping away. "More Than a Feeling" does, however, provide us glimpses of something transcendent.

STAIRWAY TO HEAVEN

Led Zeppelin

FROM THE 1971 ALBUM, LED ZEPPELIN IV

SHEET MUSIC

Culturally speaking, there's something grand that occurs when a band of Led Zeppelin's stature—apparently with the world at its fingertips—pauses to acknowledge some deeper truth through its art.

The album commonly referred to as Led Zeppelin IV has no title appearing anywhere on its cover art. Sometimes called The Fourth Album or Four Symbols, even band members do not agree on what it should be called.

"Stairway to Heaven" remains one of the most requested songs of all time. Many of the industry's trade magazines annually rate it—even more than 20 years after its release—as one of the greatest songs. But why? Does anyone even know what "Stairway to Heaven" is about?

14. Why do you think "Stairway to Heaven" would be one of the most popular songs of the modern music era?

15. Read the first verse below. What do you think connects "Stairway to Heaven" to the Larger Story? What do you think this lady wants?

There's a lady who's sure all that glitters is gold
And she's buying a stairway to heaven.
When she gets there she knows, if the stores are all closed
With a word she can get what she came for.

STAIRWAY TO HEAVEN

16. "Stairway to Heaven" is loaded with metaphorical language. What do you think it is about the language of the song that makes it so appealing? Read the passage from Colossians below. What do you think it is about mystery that stirs and awakens desire?

> There's a feeling I get when I look to the west,
> And my spirit is crying for leaving.
> In my thoughts I have seen rings of smoke through the trees,
> And the voices of those who stand looking.
> Ooh, it makes me wonder
> Ooh, it really makes me wonder
> **STAIRWAY TO HEAVEN**

> that is, the church. [25] I have become its minister, according to God's administration that was given to me for you, to make God's message fully known, [26] the ***mystery*** hidden for ages and generations but now revealed to His saints.
> **COLOSSIANS 1:24-26, EMPHASIS ADDED (HCSB)**

There are threads of desire misdirected, desire deferred, and desire awakened throughout "Stairway to Heaven". The notion that a lady believes she'll be buying her way to heaven is both tragic and inspiring at the same time. On the one hand, "buying" your way into heaven is antithetical to desire and unbiblical. On the other hand, however, the stairway—even on the whispering wind—acknowledges the heart's awareness of "something else."

IRIS

Goo Goo Dolls

FROM THE 1998 ALBUM, DIZZY UP THE GIRL

The Goo Goo Dolls are among the most successful artists in Adult Top 40 history.

SHEET MUSIC

17. Read Deuteronomy 8:2-3 below. How do you think God can use our desert experiences—adversity, emotional lows, loss—to awaken desire within us?

> And you can't fight the tears that ain't coming
> Or the moment of truth in your lies
> When everything's made to be broken
> I just want you to know who I am
>
> IRIS

> ²Remember that the LORD your God led you on the entire journey these 40 years in the wilderness, so that He might humble you and test you to know what was in your heart, whether or not you would keep His commands. ³He humbled you by letting you go hungry; then He gave you manna to eat, which you and your fathers had not known, so that you might learn that man does not live on bread alone but on every word that comes from the mouth of the LORD.
>
> DEUTERONOMY 8:2-3 (HCSB)

18. How seriously do you think God takes it when our desire is wounded or even killed?

And I don't want the world to see me
'Cause I don't think that they'd understand
IRIS

My people are broken—shattered!—and they put on Band-Aids, Saying, 'It's not so bad. You'll be just fine.' But things are not 'just fine'!
JEREMIAH 6:13 (THE MESSAGE)

INWARD AND UPWARD

Take a minute or so to reflect on the things we talked about tonight, the songs we heard, and allow God to speak into your desire. It might be that you wear your desire on your sleeve before God, but it might be that you've been ashamed or embarrassed to tell Him that you long for more—perhaps even after years of believing. In this written prayer, tell God your deepest desires.

REWIND

"Dream On"
Aerosmith

"Hungry Heart"
Bruce Springsteen

"Message in a Bottle"
The Police

REHEARSAL

Plan to spend the next meeting unpacking a few songs of lament. The lament is one of the oldest musical traditions. In fact, many of the psalms in the Bible are laments. Why is there such a basic and enduring need to express ourselves in this way? Why has this genre endured for so long? Before next week, find time to listen to the next set list and prayerfully consider humanity's need to express a sacred sorrow.

"Ironic"
Alanis Morissette

"American Pie"
Don Mclean

"Yesterday"
The Beatles

"What's Going On"
Marvin Gaye

LAMENT

SONGS OF LONGING

SETTING THE STAGE

There's a terrible misconception in many churches that Christians are not supposed to be sad—that the promises of joy and peace should be enough to "turn those frowns upside down." Nothing could be further from the truth. In fact, the Israelites were downright comfortable with letting their cries out before the Lord. There is even an entire Old Testament book devoted to these lamentations. In fact, much of Old Testament poetry (Psalms, Job, Habbakuk, Jeremiah) is made up of these songs about loss.

Jeremiah 6:16 tell us to "...stand at the crossroads and ask for the ancient paths." Lament is a part of the ancient path; it's a part of the story of humanity—especially Job, David, Jeremiah, and Jesus. The word lament, traditionally, suggests a transition or turning point. In the Larger Story, the laments of Israel were turned to joy in the promise of Christ, and the mourning of the Church will be turned to joy by His Second Coming. In the lament we are reminded of both what has been lost (Eden) and what is to come (Heaven). When we reach the point of lament, we find God waiting.

Much of popular music is made up of songs about loss. These are the sad songs. What is it about a sad song that makes us want to turn it up? Isn't that a little morbid? Or is it that there is comfort in knowing someone else has gone through it? The great songwriters tap into that experience and remind us that in the midst of loss, there is hope.

As Elton John sings, "Sad songs say so much."

> [1]There is an occasion for everything, and a time for every activity under heaven: ...[4]a time to weep and a time to laugh; a time to mourn and a time to dance.
>
> ECCLESIASTES 3:1,4 (HCSB)

1.   How do you think a lament can work as a turning point?

2.   In what ways do you think the lament is part of the human story?

BEFORE JOINING THE STORY IN SONG:
- Ask God to speak to you and reveal more of His heart to you in this time.
- Pay attention to what moves you. Is is the tone of the guitar? The emotion in the vocals? The rhythmic elements? Be aware of the moments when you feel something more.
- Consider your capacity to "feel" deeply.

SET LIST

"American Pie"
Don Mclean

"Yesterday"
The Beatles

"What's Going On"
Marvin Gaye

"Ironic"
Alanis Morissette

FROM THE 1971 ALBUM, AMERICAN PIE

SHEET MUSIC

The songwriter is grieving the loss of three rock-n-roll legends: Buddy Holly, Ritchie Valens, and the Big Bopper. "American Pie" laments the passing of significance.

3. Why do you think we tend to embrace larger-than-life personalities—people we've never met—and grieve their loss? What does this aspect of our culture say about the needs of our hearts?

4. In the passage below, why do you think the song refers to broken church bells?

> And in the streets: the children screamed,
> The lovers cried, and the poets dreamed.
> But not a word was spoken;
> The church bells all were broken.
>
> AMERICAN PIE

5. Read Lamentations 3:22-24. This verse is surrounded in the Book of Lamentations by grief, loss, and sorrow. What do you think this says about the destinations of our lamentations?

> The unfailing love of the LORD never ends! By his mercies
> we have been kept from complete destruction. 23Great is his
> faithfulness; his mercies begin afresh each day. I say to myself,
> "The LORD is my inheritance; therefore, I will hope in him!"
>
> LAMENTATIONS 3:22-24 (NLT)

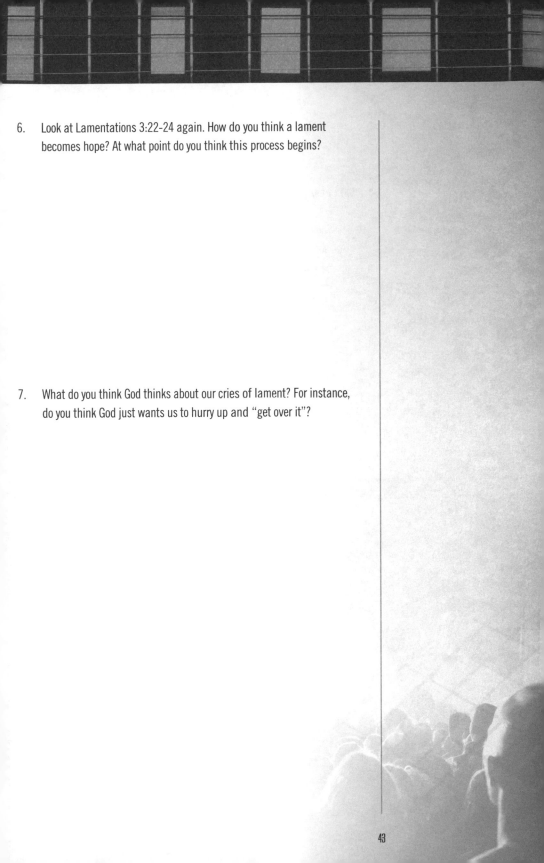

6. Look at Lamentations 3:22-24 again. How do you think a lament becomes hope? At what point do you think this process begins?

7. What do you think God thinks about our cries of lament? For instance, do you think God just wants us to hurry up and "get over it"?

FROM THE 1965 ALBUM, HELP!

 SHEET MUSIC

"Yesterday" is generally assumed to be the most covered song of all time.

"Yesterday" is a lament of what was. It's about looking back, the pain of a memory, and overcoming grief. As a classic lament of what was and still could be, you will likely recognize recurring themes.

8. The song describes the condition that has resulted from a mistake. The shadow mentioned below "hangs" which suggests some sort of permanence. What do you think this says about our tendency to dwell in regret?

> Suddenly
> I`m not half the man I used to be
> there`s a shadow hanging over me
> Oh yesterday came suddenly
> **YESTERDAY**

9. Do you think it can be emotionally healthy to lament? Why or why not?

10. Read Philippians 3:7-9 below. Describe the difference between dwelling in regret and remaining in the pain long enough to hear God.

[7]I once thought all these things were so very important, but now I consider them worthless because of what Christ has done. [8]Yes, everything else is worthless when compared with the priceless gain of knowing Christ Jesus my Lord. I have discarded everything else, counting it all as garbage, so that I may have Christ [9]and become one with him.

PHILIPPIANS 3:7-9 (NLT)

Again, this song could very well be a lament of paradise lost. Our hearts will recognize references to the hanging shadow as the taint of the Original Sin. As the place within us that senses the Larger Story unfolding around us, our hearts certainly understand the proclamation, "Oh I believe in yesterday," while warming at the thought of every trouble being so far away.

WHAT'S GOING ON   Marvin Gaye

FROM THE 1971 ALBUM, WHAT'S GOING ON

One of the central themes of the Larger Story is disorientation. When the "seen" physical world collides with the unseen spiritual world, the result is often remeniscent of Gaye's question—What's going on? The song laments a similar disorientation as confusion and social division take hold and our hearts are left to lament "the way things ought to be."

SHEET MUSIC

"What's Going On" is found on many top 100 songs of alltime lists.

11. Read Isaiah 65:24-25 below. Do you think God hears our cries of lament?

12. How do you think God would respond to the lyrics from "What's Going On" below?

Mother, mother
There's too many of you crying
Brother, brother, brother
There's far too many of you dying
You know we've got to find a way
To bring some lovin' here today

WHAT'S GOING ON

[24] "...Even before they call, I will answer; while they are still speaking, I will hear [25]The wolf and the lamb will feed together, and the lion will eat straw like the ox, but the serpent's food will be dust! They will not do what is evil or destroy on My entire holy mountain," says the Lord.

ISAIAH 65:24-25 (HCSB)

13. Can you relate to a lament like "What's Going On"? Describe a time in your life when this lament was applicable.

14. The question "what's going on?" resounds throughout this song, and it seems that the songwriter is trapped by confusion. What does this imply about your heart's need for clarity and peace? What do you think is being lamented in this case?

SHEET MUSIC

"Ironic" was nominated for Record of the Year in 1995.

Jagged Little Pill remains the top-selling debut album by a female vocalist in US history.

Although the name of the song is "Ironic", many fans (and non-fans alike) debate the presence of actual irony in the lyrics.

13.   Regardless of whether irony exists in this song or not, do you think there are ironies in our faith—truths that would seem to be contradictory on the surface?

It's like rain on your wedding day
It's a free ride when you've already paid
It's the good advice that you just didn't take
Who would've thought...it figures

IRONIC

"If you try to keep your life for yourself, you will lose it. But if you give up your life for me, you will find true life."

LUKE 9:23 (NLT)

14.   Why do you think this song would touch so many people?

Life has a funny way of sneaking up on you
Life has a funny, funny way of helping you out

IRONIC

48

15. Do you think there is a hint of affirmation and hope in a song so replete with disappointment and lament? Why or why not?

"Ironic" is full of twisted juxtaposition. The singer sings about expecting one thing, only to find a completely different reality—most of the time the exact opposite. Yet the tension is relieved through her vocals and the final revelation that life has "a funny way", a strange way about it. Our hearts recognize these twists and turns of the Larger Story on at least two levels, one of which is the lament. The other, however, is the hope and expectation that there is more. The heart of a believer will recognize the ironies and truly believe that God's "got it covered."

INWARD AND UPWARD

Spend five or ten minutes writing your lament to the Lord. Spend the first few minutes naming the losses and pains (fears, broken hearts, insecurities, crushed hopes, etc) you've suffered or are suffering. After naming those, try to come up with reasons to be thankful for some of them. This could feel impossible depending on your particular journey, but at the very least, we can all be thankful He's still in control. Our pain doesn't take His control away. In fact, it should make us more dependent on it.

◀◀

REWIND

"The Dance"
Garth Brooks

"A Man of Constant Sorrow"
The Soggy Bottom Boys

"A Long December"
Counting Crows

"Hotel California"
The Eagles

REHEARSAL

For your next meeting you'll need to be ready to talk about freedom. Freedom—the heart's cry—is integral to the Larger Story. The Book of Galatians reveals that is for freedom that Jesus set us free. Hebrews 12:1 tells us that it was for this job that Jesus endured the cross and the shame. Because freedom is so closely associated with the heart's recollection of Eden, it will most always leap up to join the songs of freedom. Before you meet, make a point to listen to the following set list.

"Born to Run"
Bruce Springsteen

"Come Sail Away"
Styx

"Don't Look Back"
Boston

"Kashmir"
Led Zeppelin

FREEDOM

THE HEART'S CRY

SETTING THE STAGE

The Gospel, among other things, is an announcement of a New Order. What is past is no longer, what was weak is now strong, what is foolish is now wise, and what was bound is now free. Accordingly, freedom is found only in binding ourselves to Jesus—the Hero of the Larger Story.

We were created to be free and our hearts long for freedom. Within the Larger Story are battles between good and evil, fascinating twists and turns, betrayal and intrigue, a hero, a villain, and a beauty to be rescued—you. In this battle the stakes are high, the ammo is live, and the bullets are real. And what's at stake? No less than your heart—what Jesus came to set free—bound by the villain of the Larger Story. Songs of freedom will inevitably glorify breaking out into the wide open, unhindered, and uninhibited. Between all of us and the sort of freedom that burns in every heart lie many obstacles. Some of these obstacles are of our own making, but most of them result from the clever schemes of the enemy, Satan.

> [32]Then you will know the truth, and the truth will set you free." [33]They answered him, "We are Abraham's descendants and have never been slaves of anyone. How can you say that we shall be set free?" [34]Jesus replied, "I tell you the truth, everyone who sins is a slave to sin. [35]Now a slave has no permanent place in the family, but a son belongs to it forever. [36]So if the Son sets you free, you will be free indeed.
>
> **JOHN 8:32-36 (NIV)**

1. The response given in John 8:33 is a legitimate one: "We are not slaves, how can you say that we need to be set free?" What sort of freedom do you think Jesus is talking about?

2. How do you think truth can set you free? And, if truth does set us free, then what do you think ultimately has the power to keep us in bondage?

BEFORE JOINING THE STORY IN SONG:

*   Ask God to speak to you and reveal more of His heart to you in this time.

*   Pay attention to what moves you. Is is the tone of the guitar? The emotion in the vocals? The rhythmic elements? Be aware of the moments when you feel something more.

*   Because not everyone appreciates the same instrumentation, rhythm, and vocals, look for lyrical merit in some to the selections on this set list.

SET LIST

"Born to Run"
Bruce Springsteen

"Come Sail Away"
Styx

"Don't Look Back"
Boston

"Kashmir"
Led Zeppelin

FROM THE 1975 ALBUM, BORN TO RUN

 SHEET MUSIC

This song is known to be Springsteen's final lunge at being a big-time performing artist.

Sprinsteen himself has been known to say that the song is about a very simple ambition: to get out of Asbury Park.

Appropriately grand for a song written as a final grasp at epic rock stardom, the lyrics dramatically point towards the freedom inherent in youth.

3. Describe the desperation found in the lyrics below. Rolling Stone Magazine put this song at #6 on the all-time greatest list. Given the timelessness of "Born to Run", do you think this song is really about getting out of New Jersey? Why or why not?

> Baby this town rips the bones from your back
> It's a death trap, it's a suicide rap
> We gotta get out while we're young
>
> **BORN TO RUN**

4. How do you think "Born to Run" has a broader application in the Larger Story and our desire for freedom?

5. Both the song "Born to Run" and Isaiah 61:1 refer to brokenness. Why do you think the path to freedom—the open road in "Born to Run" and healing in Isaiah—would be routed through brokenness?

The Spirit of the Lord GOD is on Me, because the LORD has anointed Me to bring good news to the poor. He has sent Me to heal the brokenhearted, to proclaim liberty to the captives, and freedom to the prisoners.

ISAIAH 61:1 (HCSB)

The highway's jammed with broken heroes on a last chance power drive
Everybody's out on the run tonight but there's no place left to hide
Together Wendy we'll live with the sadness
I'll love you with all the madness in my soul

BORN TO RUN

6. What do you think is the relationship between freedom and healing?

COME SAIL AWAY

Styx

FROM THE 1977 ALBUM, THE GRAND ILLUSION

Musically, "Come Sail Away" opens in piano-driven, ballad-like style before giving away to a roaring, guitar-laden build-up. This swings the door wide open from an easy, more mathematical melody to unbridled freedom.

SHEET MUSIC

The lyrics of "Come Sail Away" use the metaphor of a voyage of discovery and make reference to angels.

7.   When the songwriter says that he is the captain of his own ship, he is essentially saying that he wants to control his own destiny. Read Psalm 199:44-46 below. Do you think that encapsulates the essence of true freedom? Explain.

> I've got to be free, free to face the life that's ahead of me
> On board, I'm the captain, so climb aboard
> We'll search for tomorrow on every shore
> And I'll try, oh Lord, I'll try to carry on
> **COME SAIL AWAY**

> [45]I will walk about in freedom,
> for I have sought out your precepts.
> [46]I will speak of your statutes before kings
> and will not be put to shame,
> [47]for I delight in your commands
> because I love them.
> **PSALM 199:44-47 (NIV)**

8.   In what ways do you think taking responsibility of your own freedom can ultimately rob you of an adventure with God?

9. In "Come Sail Away" a group of angels extends an invitation to come sail away. How do you think this invitation is similar to what is found in John 14:13 and Luke 11:10 below?

> Jesus said … "Whatever you ask in My name, I will do it so that the Father may be glorified in the Son."
> **JOHN 14:13 (HCSB)**

> Jesus said … "For everyone who asks, receives; and he who seeks, finds; and to him who knocks, it will be opened."
> **LUKE 11:10 (NAS)**

> A gathering of angels appeared above my head
> They sang to me this song of hope, and this is what they said
> They said come sail away, come sail away
> **COME SAIL AWAY**

10. "Come Sail Away" sadly remembers a missed pot of gold, then defaults to a life for which the only ambition is just to "carry on"—merely endure. How do you think the freedom offered by Jesus defies this sort of existence?

> We live happily forever, so the story goes
> But somehow we missed out on that pot of gold
> But we'll try best that we can to carry on
> **COME SAIL AWAY**

Freedom in the Larger Story is about much more than just doing what you want to do, when you want to do it. Although these songs have withstood the test of time because they touch our heart with a hint of what it was made to be, the only true picture of freedom is found in the Bible. All other examples are only shadows of the truth.

FROM THE 1978 ALBUM, DON'T LOOK BACK

In Luke 9:62 Jesus says that no one that takes hold of the plow and looks back is fit for the kingdom of God. "Don't Look Back" describes a similar paradigm. In some respects, all forward motion is progress.

SHEET MUSIC

11. Read the lyrics and Scripture below. Do you think there's an association between freedom and personal transformation? Explain.

"Don't Look Back" reached #4 on the Billboard Hot 100 in 1978.

> [2]Don't copy the behavior and customs of this world, but let God transform you into a new person by changing the way you think. Then you will know what God wants you to do, and you will know how good and pleasing and perfect his will really is.
>
> ROMANS 12:2 (NLT)

> there must be a spiritual renewal of your thoughts and attitudes. You must display a new nature because you are a new person, created in God's likeness—righteous, holy, and true.
>
> EPHESIANS 4:23-24 (NLT)

> I can see
> It took so long to realize
> I'm much too strong
> Not to compromise
> Now I see what I am is holding me down
> I'll turn it around
> ***
> It's a new horizon and I'm awakin' now
> Oh I see myself in a brand new way
> The sun is shinin'
> the clouds are breakin'
>
> DON'T LOOK BACK

KASHMIR Led Zeppelin

FROM THE 1975 ALBUM, PHYSICAL GRAFFITI

SHEET MUSIC

Widely regarded as the definitive Led Zeppelin song, "Kashmir" is characterized by a driving drum line and remarkable intensity. But what makes "Kashmir" special is the different beat between the guitar and drums. This effect creates the sense of something being "loosed" or free. "Kashmir" defies formula.

12. How do the words below capture your imagination? How do think this compares to the ultimate freedom a believer can expect to find in heaven? Be specific.

> I am a traveler of both time and space, to be where I have been
> To sit with elders of the gentle race, this world has seldom seen
>
> KASHMIR

All four Led Zeppelin band members agree that "Kashmir" is one of their greatest achievements.

"Kashmir" runs for 8:28, normally a song duration too long for radio although radio stations have never had a problem playing it.

13. In what ways do you think you could be a "spiritual" traveler on a journey like the one described in "Kashmir"? Do you think being a spiritual traveler would be helpful to a person living with a heart that's come alive in the Larger Story? Explain.

14. Read the passage from Romans below. How do you think "Kashmir" metaphorically points to a place on the other side of the events being described in this passage?

[21]All creation anticipates the day when it will join God's children in glorious freedom from death and decay. [22]For we know that all creation has been groaning as in the pains of childbirth right up to the present time. [23]And even we Christians, although we have the Holy Spirit within us as a foretaste of future glory, also groan to be released from pain and suffering. We, too, wait anxiously for that day when God will give us our full rights as his children, including the new bodies he has promised us. [24]Now that we are saved, we eagerly look forward to this freedom.

ROMANS 8:21-24 (NLT)

15. "Kashmir" refers to a "storm that leaves no trace." In what ways is this reminiscent of the unseen, or spiritual, realm of the Larger Story?

Oh, pilot of the storm who leaves no trace, like thoughts inside a dream
Heed the path that led me to that place, yellow desert stream
My shangri-la beneath the summer moon, I will return again

KASHMIR

INWARD AND UPWARD

For the next ten minutes, use the space below to write freely about God's grace how you have experienced it, when you most feel it, and when you least feel it. As you're doing this, remember a time when God took something the Enemy intended for evil and turned it around for good.

Close in prayer by thanking God for the provision for freedom and a heart with the ability to know the thrill of true freedom.

REWIND

"Broken Wings"
Mr. Mister

"Raindrops Keep Falling on My Head"
BJ Thomas

"Freedom"
George Michael

"Proud Mary"
Creedence Clearwater Revival

REHEARSAL

The Book of Amos refers to a "plumb line" that God has put amidst His people (Amos 7:8). This plumb line was a line dividing wrong from right; good from evil. There are absolutes and justice is the means by which God determines them. Both Romans 8:28 and Joel 2:25, however, tell us that God has every intention of redeeming all the bad stuff in the world. He is perfectly just, but also perfectly merciful—at the same time. During the next *Finding the Larger Story through Music* we'll be talking about songs of justice, why we need them, and why we sense something greater in their stories. Until then, try to find time to review the set list below.

"Blowin' in the Wind"
Bob Dylan

"Rain on the Scarecrow"
John Cougar Mellencamp

"Like a Rolling Stone"
Bob Dylan

"For What It's Worth"
Buffalo Springfield

JUSTICE

THE ABSOLUTE RHYTHM

SETTING THE STAGE

> I will sing of your love and justice; to you, O LORD, I will sing praise.
>
> **PSALM 101:1 (NIV)**

Singing of justice. Some people call them protest songs, but that's a little misleading. While "protest" carries the weight of the issues that come and go on winds of cultural change, "justice" carries the fullest extent of "truth"—absolute and unchanging truth. In a world full of shadows and deceit, our hearts are very aware of truth at a higher, purer level. This Larger Story level is also the place where songs of justice touch us most deeply. Songs of justice pull back the curtain to reveal something to believe in that lies beyond ourselves. Because this metaphorical curtain often veils the Larger Story, these songs of justice will allow us precious glimpses of God at work and the crucial role He has for us.

These songs champion those ill-equipped to fight on their own against the ills of our day: poverty, genocide, civil unrest, and acts of terror identify a few. The message of social justice is heard again and again in the prophecies of the Old Testament. Speaking through the prophets, God often decried the institutional forms that privileged a small elite and disenfranchised the poor.

> "I will seek the lost, and I will bring back the strayed, and I will bind up the injured, and I will strengthen the weak, and the fat and the strong I will destroy. I will feed them justice."
>
> **EZEKIEL 34:16 (NIV)**

1. Has justice typically been more of a political or spiritual concern for you? How does God's concern for justice affect how you understand justice?

2. Through the prophet Ezekiel God says that He will "feed" justice to the lost, strayed, injured, and weak. How do you think justice has the power to heal these social maladies?

BEFORE JOINING THE STORY IN SONG:

- Ask God to speak to you and reveal more of His heart to you in this time.

- Pay attention to what moves you. Is is the tone of the guitar? The emotion in the vocals? The rhythmic elements? Be aware of the moments when you feel something more.

- Musical tastes are always subjective. We don't all like the same kind of music, but we are all moved by music on some level. If any of tonight's selections just isn't getting it done, find something compelling in the lyrics or Scripture.

SET LIST

"Blowin' in the Wind"
Bob Dylan

"Rain on the Scarecrow"
John Cougar Mellencamp

"Like a Rolling Stone"
Bob Dylan

"For What It's Worth"
Buffalo Springfield

BLOWIN' IN THE WIND   Bob Dylan

FROM THE 1963 ALBUM, THE FREEWHEELIN' BOB DYLAN

SHEET MUSIC

Peter, Paul, and Mary had the first hit of this Bob Dylan song in 1963. It went to #2. Rolling Stone magazine ranked this #14 in the Top 500 songs of all time.

Pay attention to the stark instrumentation and imagine yourself being in college in 1963. Your president was just assassinated in Dallas and you have the uneasy feeling that the Soviet Union was going to invade at any time.

3. Notice how often the song asks the question "How many?" What do you think this says about our natural tendency to seek justice?

Anyone who picks up a guitar, strums a few chords, and attempts to shed some light on truth has Bob Dylan to thank. Dylan's music over the past several decades has been so influential that it has become part of some sort of a "collective unconscious."

4. What questions about justice in the world plague you? How does "Blowin' in the Wind" work as an expression of your questions?

5. Read Psalm 13:1-3 below. As the psalmist wonders aloud to God, what do you think is revealed about not only our need for justice, but the heart's acknowledgment of justice's truth and accessibility?

> ¹LORD, how long will you forget me? Forever? How long will you look the other way? ²How long must I struggle with anguish in my soul,with sorrow in my heart every day? How long will my enemy have the upper hand? ³Turn and answer me, O LORD my God!
>
> **PSALM 13:1-3 (NLT)**

6. Bob Dylan didn't just write a protest song. He asked deep, philosophical questions. What do you think this song says about justice in the Larger Story? Why do you think these simple questions could be penetrating?

> Yes, 'n' how many times can a man turn his head,
> Pretending he just doesn't see?
>
> **BLOWIN' IN THE WIND**

7. Read Isaiah 56:6-7. How do you think justice looks through God's eyes? How do you think "Blowin' in the Wind" captures the essence of God's perspective of justice?

> "Is not this the kind of fasting I have chosen: to loose the chains of injustice and untie the cords of the yoke, to set the oppressed free and break every yoke? Is it not to share your food with the hungry and to provide the poor wanderer with shelter— when you see the naked, to clothe him, and not to turn away from your own flesh and blood?"
>
> **ISAIAH 56:6-7 (NIV)**

> Yes, 'n' how many ears must one man have
> Before he can hear people cry?
> Yes, 'n' how many deaths will it take till he knows
> That too many people have died?
>
> **BLOWIN' IN THE WIND**

RAIN ON THE SCARECROW   John Mellencamp

FROM THE 1985 ALBUM, SCARECROW

Willie Nelson, Neil Young, and John Mellencamp organized the Farm Aid concert as a result of a comment Bob Dylan made about the American farmer during the 1985 Live Aid. Decades later, Farm Aid continues. They've raised awareness of the plight of the American farmer and have encouraged Americans to buy local and domestic food.

SHEET MUSIC

8.   "Rain on the Scarecrow" chronicles the existence of good people following a good God and doing good things, but still, in the final analysis, end up taking it on the chin. What do you think this says about what the systems of the world reward?

9.   The rain and blood in this song symbolically represent ruin. Describe a time when you felt the same "rain and blood" of injustice.

> Rain on the scarecrow Blood on the plow
> Rain on the scarecrow Blood on the plow
> Rain on the scarecrow Blood on the plow
> **RAIN ON THE SCARECROW**

"Rain on the Scarecrow" is the unofficial theme song to the Farm Aid organization which benefits American farmers on the brink of bankruptcy.

Reached #21 on US pop charts.

10. Matthew 5:45 makes it clear that God allows the rain to fall on the evil and the good. And Isaiah 55:7-8 also makes it clear that our understanding of His actions is limited. What, if anything, does this indicate about the differences between justice in the Larger Story and the justice of our world?

> so that you may be sons of your Father in heaven. For He causes His sun to rise on the evil and the good, and sends rain on the righteous and the unrighteous.
>
> **MATTHEW 5:45 (HCSB)**

> [7]Let the wicked abandon their way of life and the evil their way of thinking. Let them come back to GOD, who is merciful, come back to our God, who is lavish with forgiveness. [8]"I don't think the way you think. The way you work isn't the way I work." GOD'S Decree.
>
> **ISAIAH 55:7-8 (THE MESSAGE)**

11. Do you think God honors the question implied in these lyrics and stated in Psalm 74? Why or why not?

> Well there's ninety-seven crosses planted in the courthouse yard
> Ninety-seven families who lost ninety-seven farms
> I think about my grandpa and my neighbors and my name
> And some nights I feel like dyin' Like that scarecrow in the rain
> Rain on the scarecrow Blood on the plow
>
> **RAIN ON THE SCARECROW**

> [10]God, how long will the foe mock? Will the enemy insult Your name forever?[11]Why do You hold back Your hand? Stretch out Your right hand and destroy them!
>
> **PSALM 74:10-11 (HCSB)**

LIKE A ROLLING STONE   Bob Dylan

FROM THE 1965 ALBUM, HIGHWAY 61 REVISITED

"Like a Rolling Stone" acknowledges the disparity among social groups and wonders aloud about any notion of justice in the world. This song is something like an 'anthem of acknowledgment' as the heart searches for greater meaning and truth.

Dylan wrote "Like a Rolling Stone" in one day during the Woodstock Music Festival

SHEET MUSIC

11. How do you think you can cry for justice without self-appointing yourself as judge?

Rolling Stone magazine ranked "Like a Rolling Stone" as the greatest song of all-time.

12. Read Psalm 82:2-4. How do you understand your role in ensuring justice? How do you think you should discern what is justice and what isn't?

> You've gone to the finest school all right, Miss Lonely
> But you know you only used to get juiced in it
> And nobody has ever taught you how to live on the street
> And now you find out you're gonna have to get used to it
>
> How does it feel
> How does it feel
> LIKE A ROLLING STONE

²How long will you judge unjustly And show partiality to the wicked?Selah. ³Vindicate the weak and fatherless; Do justice to the afflicted and destitute. ⁴Rescue the weak and needy; Deliver them out of the hand of the wicked.

PSALM 82:2-4 (NASB)

13. What do you think Romans 3:23 reveals about our ability to be the ultimate judge?

> For all have sinned and fall short of the glory of God.
>
> **ROMANS 3:23 (HCSB)**

FOR WHAT IT'S WORTH   Buffalo Springfield

FROM THE 1967 ALBUM, BUFFALO SPRINGFIELD

SHEET MUSIC

Although there are many that assume this song was written in reaction to the Kent State shootings, "For What It's Worth" was actually written and recorded before that event. Its haunting vocals leave questions hanging in the air about the way of the world, the human condition, and justice. This aspect works with its meditative feel to create an environment for contemplation.

13. How do you think we're supposed to draw clear lines in a situation where no one is right, and everyone is wrong? How do you think incorporating our own sense of justice—as opposed to God's—might create even greater injustice?

> There's battle lines being drawn
> Nobody's right if everybody's wrong
>
> **FOR WHAT IT'S WORTH**

"For What It's Worth" appears no where in the song lyrics.

Neil Young and Stephen Stills were members of Buffalo Springfield—a band that was together only 25 months.

"For What It's Worth" is a Top 100 song in Rolling Stone magazine's The 500 Greatest Songs of All Time list.

14. Read Romans 3:25-26 below. What do you think Romans 3:25-26 does to our notions of right and wrong?

> [25]For God sent Jesus to take the punishment for our sins and to satisfy God's anger against us. We are made right with God when we believe that Jesus shed his blood, sacrificing his life for us. God was being entirely fair and just when he did not punish those who sinned in former times. [26]And he is entirely fair and just in this present time when he declares sinners to be right in his sight because they believe in Jesus.
>
> **ROMANS 3:25-26 (NLT)**

15. How do you think a relationship with Jesus affects your position on justice?

Quite simply, our understanding of ideas like justice was and remains affected by the taint of original sin. The Bible, our ultimate truth source, is the standard for justice. But understanding the Scripture is predicated at least to some degree on the Holy Spirit and on our relationship with Christ. To be right with God is to understand justice as He does.

"Won't Get Fooled Again"
The Who

"With God On Our Side"
Bob Dylan

"Bullet the Blue Sky"
U2

REHEARSAL

If asked to identify the most intimate human metaphor describing our relationship with God, you might talk about God as Father or maybe Jesus as Comforter among several others. But there's an even more intimate metaphor the Bible invites us to explore: Lover to Beloved. This metaphor can be found in the poetry of the Bible as well as the prophets. Next week you'll be looking at the songs that remind our hearts of the great romance that God has invited us into. Try to find time before our next get-together to get acquainted with the following set list.

"In Your Eyes"
Peter Gabriel

"Every Breath You Take"
The Police

"You Are the Sunshine of My Life"
Stevie Wonder

NOTES

ROMANCE

A PIECE OF THE EPIC

SETTING THE STAGE

The Greeks were known to place a stringed instrument in their windows called an eolian harp. The spring and summer breeze would blow over the strings producing a harmony much like chimes might today. Samuel Coleridge's poem "The Eolian Harp" refers to a note that hangs on the stillness of the air. In Act IV of the Larger Story (p. 4), we can imagine, hang the notes of desire, romance, lament, freedom, emptiness, and chaos—an eternal chord all at once. We've always wanted more, and the song—both music and lyric—gives a glimpse into the world of the heart.

God at His very core is a romantic and it is in the context that we can best grasp the relationship God desires with each of us. When He lets us know in the First Commandment that He is a jealous God, He is unequivocally saying that our relationship with Him is an exclusive. Given this, the gospel story that begins in Genesis in the earliest moments in the process of redemption and never ends, is the story of God's pursuit of us. This pursuit is the epic romance.

> The LORD your God is with you, he is mighty to save He will take
> great delight in you ... he will rejoice over you with singing."
> **ZEPHANIAH 3:17 (NIV)**

1.   God has been thinking about you for a long time. Why do you think this would be difficult for some—even professing belivers— to believe?

2. Zephaniah 3:17 tells us that God takes delight in us; that He rejoices over us with singing. Do you think God feels like this about you all the time? Why or why not?

BEFORE JOINING THE STORY IN SONG:

- Ask God to speak to you and reveal more of His heart to you in this time.

- Pay attention to what moves you. Is is the tone of the guitar? The emotion in the vocals? The rhythmic elements? Be aware of the moments when you feel something more.

- Remember that musical tastes are always subjective.

SET LIST

"In Your Eyes"
Peter Gabriel

"You Are the Sunshine of My Life"
Stevie Wonder

"Every Breath You Take"
The Police

IN YOUR EYES   Peter Gabriel

FROM THE 1986 ALBUM, SO

We all know the scene from *Say Anything*. An awkward Lloyd Dobler (played by John Cusack) stands outside Diane Court's window, unable to find the words to express what he wants to say. So he holds a portable stereo over his head and plays "In Your Eyes." His pursuit of her only captured in his stillness, allowing truth to unfurl.

Peter Gabriel has said this song could be about a man's relationship with a woman or a man's relationship with God.

Like many of the songs that have survived the test of time, the single only reached #26 on US pop charts.

All my instincts, they return
And the grand facade, so soon will burn
Without a noise, without my pride
I reach out from the inside

In your eyes
The light the heat,
In your eyes
I am complete
IN YOUR EYES

SHEET MUSIC

3.   The song claims that the lover's eyes are akin to a doorway—a doorway to a thousand churches. What do you think the songwriter is trying to say about the lover? What do you think this says about the lover's heart?

In your eyes
I see the doorway to a thousand churches
In your eyes
The resolution of all the fruitless searches
IN YOUR EYES

4. How do you think "In Your Eyes" integrates the secular and the sacred? What do you think this integration reveals about God's pursuit of you?

5Christ Jesus, 6who, existing in the form of God, did not consider equality with God as something to be used for His own advantage. Instead He emptied Himself by assuming the form of a slave, taking on the likeness of men. 7And when He had come as a man in His external form, He humbled Himself by becoming obedient 8to the point of death—even to death on a cross.

PHILIPPIANS 2:5-8 (HCSB)

5. To what degree have you felt pursued by God—been wooed by Him?

Love I get so lost, sometimes
Days pass and this emptiness fills my heart
When I want to run away
I drive off in my car
But whichever way I go
I come back to the place you are

IN YOUR EYES

He will be with you; He will not leave you or forsake you. Do not be afraid or discouraged.

DEUTERONOMY 31:8 (HCSB)

6. What do you think both the lyrics below and Matthew 11:28-30 say about the true nature of romance—romance in the Larger Story?

> I look to the time with you to keep me awake and alive
> **IN YOUR EYES**

> [28]"Come to Me, all of you who are weary and burdened, and I will give you rest.
> [29]All of you, take up My yoke and learn from Me, because I am gentle and humble in heart, and you will find rest for yourselves. [30]For My yoke is easy and My burden is light."
> **MATTHEW 11:28-30 (THE MESSAGE)**

YOU ARE THE SUNSHINE OF MY LIFE   Stevie Wonder

FROM THE 1973 ALBUM, TALKING BOOK

SHEET MUSIC

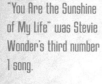

"You Are the Sunshine of My Life" was Stevie Wonder's third number 1 song.

7. Do you think this song could be one of God's songs to you? Why or why not?

> You are the sunshine of my life
> That's why I'll always stay around
> You are the apple of my eye
> For ever you'll stay in my heart
> **YOU ARE THE SUNSHINE OF MY LIFE**

> Keep me as the apple of your eye; hide me in the shadow of your wings
> **PSALM 17:8 (NIV)**

8. If you believed "You Are the Sunshine of My Life" was God's song to you, how do you think it would change your relationship with Him?

9. In addition to the the normal reading of Song of Songs as wife to husband, the Lover-Beloved relationship can also be read metaphorically as our relationship with God. Read 4:9 below. Do you think you have the ability to move God as a lover to the beloved?

You have stolen my heart, my sister, my bride; you have stolen my heart with one glance of your eyes, with one jewel of your necklace.

SONG OF SONGS 4:9 (NIV)

10. Who do you think is the rescuer in the Larger Story? Who is your redeemer?

11. Read Isaiah 61:1—also the prophecy Jesus read in Luke 4. How is Isaiah 61:1 similar to the lyrics below?

> You must have known that I was lonely
> Because you came to my rescue
> And I know that this must be heaven
> How could so much love be in side of you?
> **YOU ARE THE SUNSHINE OF MY LIFE**

> The Spirit of the Lord GOD is on Me, because the LORD has anointed Me to bring good news to the poor. He has sent Me to heal the brokenhearted, to proclaim liberty to the captives, and freedom to the prisoners
> **ISAIAH 61:1 (HCSB)**

EVERY BREATH YOU TAKE   The Police

FROM THE 1983 ALBUM, SYNCHRONICITY

"Every Breath You Take" captures the internal dialogue of a heart obsessed with another. One of the biggest hits for The Police, "Every Breath You Take" is a song about single-mindedness. It reminds us that God has been thinking about us for a long time.

SHEET MUSIC

12. Do you think obsessing over a person is healthy, or do you tend to think it to be unhealthy?

> Every breath you take
> Every move you make
> Every single day
> Every word you say
> **EVERY BREATH YOU TAKE**

"Every Breath You Take" ranks #84 on the Rolling Stone list of the Top 500 Greatest Songs of All Time..

13. Read Matthew 10:30. Do you think it could be possible that God might obsess over you? Discuss.

> He pays even greater attention to you, down to the last detail—even numbering the hairs on your head!
>
> **MATTHEW 10:30 (THE MESSAGE)**

It is true that God has been thinking about you for a long time. (See Jeremiah 1:5.) The God-character in *The Shack*, a fictitious account of the Trinity, says several times, "I'm especially fond of him," or "I'm especially fond of her." Yet each time a different person is being identified. The point is that God is especially fond of everyone. Does He obsess? Well, why not. Maybe God still has some surprises for us.

Too often we make the mistake of heaping our definitions with all their baggage onto the divine relationship with God. In this particular case, doing so can taint the beautiful image of God as the gentle, kind lover. The Larger Story requires passion. It inspires romance. If we, as God's image bearers, long for romance, then you can be sure that there is a romantic aspect to God as well. It's this side of Him just as much as any other that is behind Jesus' daring rescue mission into enemy territory.

INWARD AND UPWARD

If there were a love song written about you and your relationship with God, what would it be? It can be you singing to God, or God singing to you. Feel free to use a song we discussed tonight, but describe in detail why you and the Lord would call it "our song."

"Wonderful Tonight"
Eric Clapton

"Unchained Melody"
Righteous Brothers

"In My Life"
The Beatles

"My Girl"
The Temptations

WELCOME TO COMMUNITY

WELCOME TO COMMUNITY!

Meeting together with a group of people to study God's Word and experience life together is an exciting adventure. A small group is ... a group of people unwilling to settle for anything less than redemptive community.

CORE VALUES

COMMUNITY

God is relational, so He created us to live in relationship with Him and each other. Authentic community involves sharing life together and connecting on many levels with the people in our group.

GROUP PROCESS

Developing authentic community requires a step-by-step process. It's a journey of sharing our stories with each other and learning together.

STAGES OF DEVELOPMENT

Every healthy group goes through various stages as it matures over a period of months or years. We begin with the birth of a new group, deepen our relationships in the growth and development stages, and ultimately multiply to form other new groups.

INTERACTIVE BIBLE STUDY

God provided the Bible as an instruction manual of life. We need to deepen our understanding of God's Word. People learn and remember more as they wrestle with truth and learn from others. The process of Bible discovery and group interaction will enhance our growth.

EXPERIENTIAL GROWTH

The goal of studying the Bible together is not merely a quest for knowledge; this should result in real life change. Beyond solely reading, studying, and dissecting the Bible, being a disciple of Christ involves reunifying knowledge with experience. We do this by bringing our questions to God, opening a dialogue with our hearts (instead of killing our desires), and utilizing other ways to listen to God speak to us (group interaction, nature, art, movies, circumstances, etc.). Experiential growth is always grounded in the Bible as God's primary means of revelation and our ultimate truth-source.

THE POWER OF GOD

Our processes and strategies will be ineffective unless we invite and embrace the presence and power of God. In order to experience community and growth, Jesus needs to be the centerpiece of our group experiences and the Holy Spirit must be at work.

REDEMPTIVE COMMUNITY

Healing best happens within the context of community and in relationship. A key aspect of our spiritual development is seeing ourselves through the eyes of others, sharing our stories, and ultimately being set free from the secrets and the lies we embrace that enslave our souls.

MISSION

God has invited us into a larger story with a great mission. It is a mission that involves setting captives free and healing the broken-hearted (Isaiah 61:1-2). However, we can only join in this mission to the degree that we've let Jesus bind up our wounds and set us free. As a group experiences true redemptive community, other people will be attracted to that group, and through that group to Jesus. We should be alert to inviting others while we maintain (and continue to fill) an "empty chair" in our meetings to remind us of others who need to encounter God and authentic Christian community.

SHARING YOUR STORIES

The sessions in *Finding the Larger Story through Music* are designed to help you share a little of your personal lives with the other people in your group. Through your time together, each member of the group is encouraged to move from low risk, less personal sharing to higher risk communication. Real community will not develop apart from increasing intimacy of the group over time.

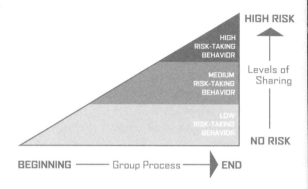

SHARING YOUR LIVES

As you share your lives together during this time, it is important to recognize that it is God who has brought each person to this group, gifting the individuals to play a vital role in the group (1 Corinthians 12:1). Each of you has been uniquely designed to contribute in your own unique way to building into the lives of the other people in your group. As you get to know one another better, consider the following four areas that will be unique for each person. These areas will help you get a "grip" on how you can better support others and how they can support you.

G — **Spiritual Gifts**: God has given you unique spiritual gifts (1 Corinthians 12; Romans 12:3-8; Ephesians 4:1-16; etc.).

R — **Resources**: You have resources that perhaps only you can share, including skill, abilities, possessions, money, and time (Acts 2:44-47; Ecclesiastes 4:9-12, etc.).

I — **Individual Experiences**: You have past experiences, both good and bad, that God can use to strengthen others (2 Corinthians 1:3-7; Romans 8:28, etc.).

P — **Passions**: There are things that excite and motivate you. God has given you those desires and passions to use for His purposes (Psalm 37:4,23; Proverbs 3:5-6,13-18; etc.).

To better understand how a group should function and develop in these four areas, consider going through the Serendipity study entitled *Great Beginnings*.

LEADING A SMALL GROUP

LEADING A SMALL GROUP

You will find a great deal of helpful information in this section that will be crucial for success as you lead your group.

Reading through this and utilizing the suggested principles and practices will greatly enhance the group experience. You need to accept the limitations of leadership. You cannot transform a life. You must lead your group to the Bible, the Holy Spirit, and the power of Christian community. By doing so your group will have all the tools necessary to draw closer to God and each other, and to experiencing heart transformation.

Make the following things available at each session:

- *Finding the Larger Story through Music* study for each attendee

- Bible for each attendee

- Snacks and refreshments

- Pens or pencils for each attendee

THE SETTING AND GENERAL TIPS

1. Prepare for each meeting by reviewing the material, praying for each group member, asking the Holy Spirit to join you, and making Jesus the centerpiece of every experience.

2. Create the right environment. Set the room temperature at 69 degrees and make sure pets are in a location where they cannot interrupt the meeting. Have music playing as people arrive (volume low enough for people to converse) and, if possible, burn a sweet-smelling candle.

3. Try to have soft drinks and coffee available for early arrivals.

4. Have someone with the spiritual gift of hospitality ready to make any new attendees feel welcome.

5. Be sure there is adequate lighting so that everyone can read without straining.

6. There are four types of questions used in each session: Observation (What is the passage telling us?), Interpretation (What does the passage mean?), Self-revelation (How am I doing in light of the truth unveiled?), and Application (Now that I know what I know, what will I do to integrate this truth into my life?). You won't be able to use all the questions in each study, but be sure to use some from each.

7. Connect with group members away from group time. The amount of participation you have during your group meetings is directly related to the amount of time you connect with your group members away from the meeting time.

8. Don't get impatient about the depth of relationship group members are experiencing. Building real Christian community takes time.

9. Be sure pens and/or pencils are available for attendees at each meeting.

10. Never ask someone to pray aloud without first getting their permission.

LEADING MEETINGS

1. The meeting should feel like a conversation from beginning to end, not a classroom experience.

2. Be certain every member responds to the session introductory questions. The goal is for every person to hear his or her own voice early in the meeting. People will then feel comfortable to converse later on. If members can't think of a response, let them know you'll come back to them after the others have spoken.

3. Remember, a great group leader talks less than 10% of the time. If you ask a question and no one answers, just wait. If you create an environment where you fill the gaps of silence, the group will quickly learn they needn't join you in the conversation.

4. Don't be hesitant to call people by name as you ask them to respond to questions or to give their opinions. Be sensitive, but engage everyone in the conversation.

5. Don't ask people to read aloud unless you have gotten their permission prior to the meeting. Feel free to ask for volunteers to read.

6. Watch your time. If discussion time is extending past the time limits suggested, offer to the option of pressing on into other discussions or continuing the current session into your next meeting. REMEMBER: People and their needs are always more important than completing all the questions.

THE GROUP

Each small group has it's own persona. Every group is made up of a unique set of personalities, backgrounds, and life experiences. This diversity creates a dynamic distinctive to that specific group of people. Embracing the unique character of your group and the individuals in that group is vital to group members experiencing all you're hoping for.

Treat each person as special, responsible, and valuable members of this Christian community. By doing so you'll bring out the best in each of them, thus creating a living, breathing, life-changing group dynamic.

YOU CAN HELP GROUP MEMBERS THROUGH ...

Support
Provide plenty of time for support among the group members. Encourage members to connect with each other between meetings as they can.

Shared Feelings
Reassure the members that their feelings are very normal in a situation such as they are in. Encourage the members to share their feelings with one another.

Advice Giving
Avoid giving advice. Encourage cross-talk (members talking to each other), but limit advice giving. "Should" and "ought" to statements tend to increase the guilt the loss has already created.

Silence
Silence is not a problem. Even though it may seem awkward, silence is just a sign that people are not ready to talk. It DOES NOT mean they aren't thinking or feeling. If the silence needs to be broken, be sure you break it with the desire to move forward.

Prayer
Prayer is vital to personal and community growth. Starting and ending with prayer is important. However, people may need prayer in the middle of the session. Here's a way to know when the time is right to pray. If a member is sharing and you sense a need to pray, then begin to look for a place to add it.

NOTES

GOD & THE ARTS

Where faith intersects life.

The *God and the Arts* series includes *Finding Jesus in the Movies* and *Finding Redemption in the Movies*. This study reveals how great movies echo the larger story alive in the heart of us all. Movies to view include *Seabiscuit, Gladiator, Signs,* and *An Unfinished Life.* Your small group will discover through story a deeper understanding of the larger story and the significant role for each of us.

Finding Redemption in the Movies
1574943421

Finding Jesus in the Movies
1574943553

FOUNDATIONS

Experience the mystery for the first time. Again.

Jesus seemed to love paradox and often taught by asking questions rather than dumping information. It's an idea we can all connect with—an idea we all struggle with. At some point in our lives, we've had questions—"Who is God" and "Where was He when...". God can handle these questions and desires the intimacy that comes from working through them. *The Foundations of the Faith* series takes groups through this process.

Foundational Truths
1574943111

Knowing Jesus
1574943103

The Christian in a Postmodern World
1574941089

God and the Journey to Truth
1574941097

experiences
from Serendipity House...

CANVAS

A DVD-driven small-group experience.

Emerging inside each of us is a unique work of art that reveals who we are and our vital role in the larger story. *Canvas* has been created to draw from deep within the stories God has given each of us, and to expose the beauty God is forging from the sum of our experiences. Using the power of story and art through DVD's and an Experience Guide for each group member, this small-group series brings a new multi-media dimension to Bible study. *Canvas* provides the context, the texture, and the materials for the journey. Through your story, your experiences, and the colors of your reality, God works to bring your role in the larger story to light.

DISTORTIONS	MYSTERY	HEART
Kit 1574943367	Kit. 1574943561	Kit 1574943588
Experience Guide .1574943375	Experience Guide . 157494357X	Experience Guide . .1574943596

ACKNOWLEDGMENTS

We pray that God will work through your time together to reveal the crucial role you have been called and created to fill in the Larger Story—an epic more real than the physical world we inhabit. Serendipity House would like to acknowledge the following for their roles in completing *Finding the Larger Story in Music*.

Contributing Writers
Brian Daniel
Barry Cram
Randy Williams

Cover + Interior Design
Brian Marschall